Every Single Thing

Every Single Thing

Joanie McLean

© 2021 TEXT, JOANIE MCLEAN

Wayfarer Books supports copyright. Copyright fuels creativity, encourages diverse voices, promotes free speech, and creates a vibrant culture. Thank you for buying an authorized edition of this book and for complying with copyright laws by not reproducing, scanning, or distributing any part of it in any form without permission. You are supporting writers and allowing Wayfarer Books to continue to publish books for every reader.

Quantity sales: Special discounts are available on quantity purchases by corporations, associations, bookstores, and others. For details, contact the publisher or visit wholesalers such as Ingram or Baker & Taylor.

All Rights Reserved
Published in 2021 by Wayfarer Books
Cover Design and Interior Design by Leslie M. Browning
Cover Painting "Icy Creek on the Haw" by Jane Eckenrode | janeeckenrode.com
First Edition Trade Paperback 978-1-953340-40-5

10 9 8 7 6 5 4 3 2 1

Look for our titles in paperback, ebook, and audiobook wherever books are sold. Wholesale offerings for retailers available through Ingram at the trade discount.

Wayfarer Books is committed to ecological stewardship. We greatly value the natural environment and invest in environmental conservation.

For Heather McIver, L.Ac.
A true healer

ALSO BY THE AUTHOR

Up From Dust

Place

TABLE OF CONTENTS

I. FARM NOTES

...as though my life depends...
- 5 Just Before Dawn
- 6 Fox in the Field at Sunset
- 7 Calf
- 8 Coyote Brings Dawn
- 9 Hard Winter
- 11 Niche

...what makes the horses gallop so...
- 15 I Wake in the Night
- 16 Reconcile
- 18 Feeding the Horses
- 19 Winter's Claim
- 20 Snow Coming
- 22 Tell Me
- 24 Down
- 26 For Now

...here I am. Take me, too...
- 31 Mergansers
- 33 Black Mingo Creek
- 35 The Fish
- 36 Rabbit
- 37 Beetle Life
- 39 Gamagrass
- 40 Crickets

...I wonder if you know...

    45 Traveling

    47 Haunt

    49 Do You Know

    50 Grief, Still

    52 I Live Alone Now

    54 Times Like This

II. SKIMMERS

...the lift and glide...

    61 Still Don't Understand

    62 And Yet

    63 The Geese Are Back

    64 Wings of Owls

    65 Drought

    66 Skimmers

    67 Bird Woman

    68 Wood Duck Calls

...it must be all right...

    73 Things Noted on the Way to Town

    74 It Must Be All Right

    76 Waiting for the Kindling to Catch

    78 Down to the Bone

    80 Addressing Climate Change

    82 Agalinis

    84 Letter to a Great Grandson

    85 What's Left

...to let go every single thing...
- 89 Field Weeds, Winter Coming
- 90 Hickory
- 91 Abscission
- 92 Would Go, Too
- 93 Will Not Tell
- 95 One Single Thing
- 96 Potatoes and Sparrows and Wind
- 97 Sweet Coming Apart
- 99 Remember This

Acknowledgements
About the Author
About the Publisher

I. FARM NOTES

...as though my life depends...

JUST BEFORE DAWN

Against the darkest hour
a wisp of smoke,
two yellow-green globes
turn towards me
at the sound
of my shoulder shifting
against
the side of the barn.
The fox squats
marks her trail
along the garden fence
to the compost heap
her eyes holding mine
as though my life depends
on these moments
when their wild cold glow
floats through
my smoothed and fenced farm
at this uncanny hour
when the world
comes unglued
from its page
shifts and glides
where we think it wouldn't.
And it does,
it does.

FOX IN THE FIELD AT SUNSET

If I could lie down
in the rustly weeds
with you,
pressed against
the stubble and mud,
I would bring
my face so close
to yours,
your silver
whiskers would twitch
and spring as though
they are mine.

And I would hear the naked
mouse babies cry
in the next field over.

To close my eyes,
to suffer a breath,
would shake me back
to human-ness.
So I am holding still
but only as still
as a human.
And so you rise
and shake your coat.
I shiver as the sun
goes down.

CALF

Just after first light
there's movement
through the tree line.
Over in the neighbor's field—
shapes in brown and grey
a flash of black.
Two coyotes move
with unmistakable intent
circling and yipping. They drag
the carcass of a calf
under the fence
into my unmown field.

They nudge and jerk at the throat—
turn on each other in their delight,
bare teeth, grin—then back to the bloody calf.

I hear a four-wheeler
along the fence line—
my neighbor coming
to check his herd, to check
the pregnant heifers.
That sudden breeze
that always precedes
the sun's arrival
ruffles the coyotes' coats,
rippling their silver-tipped hairs
like wind through a grain field.

COYOTE BRINGS DAWN

coyote grins
with kohl-lined eyes and lips
side-winding hindquarters
syncopate his lope
across ice-white fields
nosing under
the hot wire
he slides a clump
of horse dung
out across
the frozen crust
lowers a shoulder
onto the prize
caressing it
with neck and jaw
peach and white
of belly flash
he springs up
sniffs the dung
and when he shakes
the field crackles
with snow stars
dawn leaps
to the horizon

HARD WINTER

Looking up from my desk
midmorning, I see the coyote pair
crossing the back meadow
as they often do. But
something's amiss—
it's not their time
to be abroad,
and the big male
is limping heavily.
Something in the light
is wrong.
As he lopes
across the snow
he casts
a bloody shadow.
The female's following
is hesitant.
She starts and stops, drops
her head low.
Shoulder blades flaring,
she runs behind him
at a crouch.
When they reach the pond
he sniffs the ice, paws at its edge,
raises his head, then tries the surface again.

They both squint
into the wind
that skates across the ice,
then slip into the shadows
at the tree line.
My eyes mark a stone
at the edge of the pond
as I rise from my desk
and reach for my coat.

NICHE

So this year
it will be the fox
who will wind and dally
across the meadow,
push forepaws and nose
into whispery mounds and burrows,
and take the sketchy paths
into the woods

paths first etched
by her counterpoint—coyote,
who crossed this meadow
a few seasons ago,
bloody in the snow,
shot for crimes so old
the shooter no longer
bothers to name them.

> *Tiny bones*
> *click and scrape*
> *in the empty den—*

.

The vixen will sniff these brittle bits,
pull her lips back, crouching
in the musky dark. She'll back out again,
scrape the earth at the entrance,
squat and make her mark.

What makes the horses gallop so....

I WAKE IN THE NIGHT

hearing hooves
against the drought-hardened hill.
    Coyotes, feral dogs, swooping night birds, the rain-laced wind I pray for
    come swinging in to fill the murky spaces of my sleep.
What makes the horses
gallop so
in this darkest hour?

I am wild with envy
for their urgency
their tearing into the night
whirling at the top of the hill
to take in all the world
and send it flying to the stars
with snorts like rifle shots.

These walls
and bed clothes
stifle me. I hold them close
and wake at dawn
to the tatting of rain
on the window sill.

RECONCILE

I remember being wheeled
into a large room,
a floor that sloped
to a drain at the center,
unfamiliar shapes in stainless steel.
Nothing else. But later
odd bits gathered
from the surgeon's comments
the physical therapist's cautions—
there must have been
a drill, likely a saw,
and a measuring instrument
of exquisite precision.
Titanium forced into bone
for a tight fit.
Muscles and fascia
stretched and cut
for expedience.

Along the farm road to the barn
the roan horse approaches cautiously,
snorting, eyeing my cane
and lurching gait.
Cicadas buzz and whir in the woods.
A phoebe on the wire tells
and tells her name. This,
and the scent of hot sun in the pines,

bring at first just tears
then wrenching and tearing
in a deeper place. But there

the phoebe still
wags and tells its name.
Later this afternoon hawks
will ride hot air
up over the pasture.
After sundown katydids
will shake and shush all night.
And then autumn
will silence them again
with its sighing and rotting.
Mingo is at the fence now,
sweet soft muzzle lipping
the palm of my hand,
remembering apples.

FEEDING THE HORSES

When rain comes sheeting
dark across the farm
even on a spring morning

and cold reaches
through your jacket
sending icy trickles

along that particular
rise and curve
of your collar bone

if memory
can be said
to assume a presence

then you'll not be alone
as you swing the pasture gate
against the wind,

fend off the impatient
mare, and fill the mangers
with hay.

WINTER'S CLAIM

I've just lighted a fire in the stove and set the coffee to making.
And so to leave the house on this sleety Sunday morning
has made a heavy claim on my fortitude. I'm headed to the barn
to hay the horses, fill their trough, and feed the cats.

There's glistening scat in the farm road telling who's come in the night.
Mingo's warm muzzle on the back of my neck as I lean to fork manure.
His ice-coated mane clinks at my cheek.

The ragged call of two herons in flight,
unhurried through the freezing mist.
They change their course to pass just over my head.

In the end, of course, whatever Winter claims
has been a paltry price to pay for such a morning.

SNOW COMING

Thunder ten days ago.
So now the sky
lowers itself over the barn,
greys up hard and grim.
The wind tests the tin roof,
tries the tack room door.
The barn cats hunker
in the crannies
between the hay bales,
watching me
cut baling twine.

I hear the horses
pounding up the frozen hill
as I fill their hay bags
against the mounting storm.
In a rush and swirl
of hooves and snorting,
they fill the barn
with their sweet scent,
shaking the first flakes
from their manes
and necks. I have tried

to imagine
what it would take
to leave this all behind—
to step up into the jagged wind,
or fade down the hill
and drift against the fence line.

Later tonight
when the storm
has satisfied itself
the field will be still
and the stars will spark
in the white snow
and in the black sky.

TELL ME

Seven degrees this morning.
The crystalline light of a sharp
winter dawn takes the eastern horizon.
The snowy pasture emerges
around the dark shapes
of cedar trees and sumac tangle.
I know this landscape by heart,
and there's one shape that's wrong.
Sunny, the old chestnut gelding,
is down again. Colic for sure, again.

> *Wool tights, down vest, head lamp, whatever gloves come to hand*
> *Run if you can   along the frozen wheel tracks to the barn*
> *Cut the power to the fence   put the Banamine in your pants to warm*
> *Whatever you do don't take off your gloves*
> *Take the blue halter—the only one big enough for Sunny*

He's on his side, lifts his head as I approach.
His blond tail is dark, slick with excrement.
But it is his eye—filmy, unfocused,
with nothing to say this time—
that holds me.

He's shivering, and he's old,
and he must not stay down.
He allows the halter.
I let him say when.

Then I pull so he won't
change his mind.
He's up.

We head toward the barn—
I slide along the frozen crust,
he breaks through with each step.
It's full light now. Sunny stumbles.
I watch his eye. That's how he'll tell me.
He'll need to tell me
which way he's going this time.

DOWN

Sunny is gone now.
We called the vet to
euthanize him, put him down.
An apt expression in the case
of a horse. The first injection
brought his head down. Then

he knelt on the frozen ground
into the sparkling grass.

We had led him

to the top of the hill against
the woods where we could turn
and see the whole farm.
The other horses had
followed at a distance, curious
about the waiting backhoe.

Sunny slumped onto his side.

The vet stood at her truck, handling
syringe and vials. I tangled
my fingers through the hank of mane
in my pocket, stumbled
over sumac stobs on the way back
to the barn. Behind me

up on the hill our neighbor started his backhoe.

I went back up the hill one more time
when the pile of earth looked
about right. Down
in that hole what I saw
affirmed that the horse was gone.
But where, I couldn't say.

FOR NOW

The way old fields lie
here in the Piedmont,
give down slopes
of hay scent,
push through sloughs
of blackberry and beggar tick,
pull up at the top
of a rise.

The meager trails
that horses make
take what's offered
along sketchy contours
or a modest ridge.
Dirt and grass
certain under foot,
breeze deft across the face

so that for now it's safe
to look up and out
over the field
where an ordinary life
spreads away from you
like a wake trailing the afternoon sun
and you wonder how a field
could know such things.

...here I am. Take me, too...

MERGANSERS

I spot them
fishing in the bully charge
of the river's current.
From the center of the bridge
I watch them spring up
upon the surface
toss their heads
fling icelets
from their iridescent
necks.

I've come here
just ahead of the sleet
to see if they're okay.
To see how
they can be okay.
They dive and rise
dive and rise
amidst fingers of ice
that reach from the rocks
into the current.
I am paralyzed
by their ordeal.

I conjure what I know
of oiled feathers
and layers of fat.

I touch my bare neck,
consider
the distance down.
A steady wind brings tears,
streams them back
into my ears and hair.
The iron rail
has ignored my gloves
and frozen my fingers.

I watch the male
collapse his crest
then fan it out—white
against the dark bank.
Sleet ticks.
The rapids
suck and breathe
behind me.

BLACK MINGO CREEK

Evening
slants along
through the canopy
of red and gold,
tupelo gum and water hickory.
Light and leaves
afloat among the trees,
my boat afloat
in this rusty
current
that slithers
deftly round hair-pin turns
and switch-back loops,
slides into
the murky dim
always
just ahead.
Slick black
widow-maker logs
rise and nose the current,
nudge my boat,
scratch their fingers
along its sides.
Cooters and sliders,
soaking up the last weak rays
of the shortening days,

lumber along their logs
and abandon ship,
announcing
my approach
to the coven
of cotton mouths
coiled on the mucky shore.
My boat in the current
goes silent,
my heart waits—
I nod my respect
towards the shore,
"Evenin' ma'ams."

THE FISH

Standing at the kitchen sink
I happen to glance up:
out across the deck and dunes
the unmistakable flash
of white and black—
a bald eagle skims the surf.
His yellow talons
reach forward and down
into the roiling waves.

    I run to the porch, out onto the deck,
    shading my eyes with a slimy hand
    that smells of grocery meat and onions.

The arc of his pass—
from sky to sea to sky again—
smooth and unbroken as he lifts
the stunned and streaming fish
to glint in the hard air.
His eye unblinking, his beak agape,
the eagle passes silent over the house,
heading back across the neck to the river.
I turn in his wake. Here I am.
Take me. Take me, too.

RABBIT

What might I have done
to see you sooner,
a few seconds to brake
hard enough
to parse your zig-zags
up the center of the road.
On my way back
I see that other drivers
have not bothered to avoid
your carcass.

Once
a wood duck
shot up out of the reeds
so close and sudden
that I saw its throat
quaver as it cried out,
its red eye fixed to mine.
There was no distance
in that instant
between our two startled hearts.

So maybe what left you, rabbit —
here on Silk Hope Road
at 5:30 this morning—
maybe what left you was only
that furry, silky, downy pelt,
that smear of red and purple,
those white tendons.

BEETLE LIFE

Lady bugs litter the rug,
are scattered across the bed
where they have bailed
out of the overhead light.
Through the winter months
I try each orange carapace
for life, place a monstrous finger
against the hardened forewing,
testing for response.

If no movement ensues—
no jointed leg extends,
no wing case
opens down the back—
I conclude that
this one's dead,
pinch the papery
exoskeleton up,
add it to the compost.

Sometimes I'm mistaken
and brittle little legs
scrabble against my thumb.
In that moment, a tiny flash
of light, or is it shadow—
whatever I'd been

weighing odds against,
what I'd decided
wasn't there—
asserts itself against
my clumsy mind, this heart
that I've neglected.

GAMAGRASS

If I had gone to town
for the paper this morning

I would not be down here
among the gamagrass blades
watching their seed pods arch
out over the pond,
hoping to witness
the desiccation
the peeling back
of the supple sheaths,
the spilling of tawny
cylindrical seeds
like tiny vertebrae
coming undone.

I would not be here
as the snapping turtle
rises and huffs
rubs his ancient brow
against the muddy bank.

CRICKETS

It's crickets now,
whirring with offbeat rhythm.
The cicada's buzz,
the katydid's rattle
have gone,
following Summer
as she moved on.
She closed up camp
just yesterday morning.
I watched her from the barn.
She shaded her eyes
as she looked east
to measure the angle
of morning light,
then turned and gathered
a few loose ends—
late blooming asters,
muhlie grass plumes—
into her satchel.
She smiled and hummed,
pushed straw hair
off her tanned face,
and walked out of the meadow.
I believe
she looked wistful,
but she never looked back.
So it's crickets now.

...I wonder if you know...

TRAVELING

Already a year
since we stood watch
as you slipped away.
First you couldn't swallow.
We learned to be gentle
with the suction. The one time
sobbing came upon you
panic rose quietly
in your eyes
as you began to drown,
so you put away
whatever it was —
thoughts of your babies,
all that was left
unpaid or unfinished,

Later on
speaking went,
then nodding,
then opening your eyes.
We had no way
to know you after that.
We knew your body though,
turning it, cleaning it, learning
its emptiness.
Never sure of what was left,
of what was still you.

We moved you to the porch,
October's brilliance
thrilling us by day,
its first chill evenings
rendering us transparent
so that for some time
we traveled with you
while you disappeared.

HAUNT

There's that sound
on the steps.
Of course
you'd be here—
what with a day
like this one
has been. The sky's
terrific blue,
the jump and swing
of the surf,
and then
the startling
appearance
of the moon
full and red
stepping up
over the distance
onto the ruched sea.

It's not footsteps
that I hear,
not the creak
of old cypress treads.
Just the sound
of air against air.
There's barely a breeze
off the ocean tonight—

no, yours
is a closer sound.
I crane from my bed
towards the stairwell
for sigh or
brush of cloth
against skin,
for intimation
of what you've become.

Do you still sit
on the bench
at the top
of the dunes.
Did you love
this beautiful day.

I try to count the steps
as you come.
I know there are ten.
I wonder
if you know
that it's me
who's here.

DO YOU KNOW

that I carried your
little boy last night
through the crowd
at the annual Christmas party—
the party you had thrown for years,
the one the whole town turned out for.
Oysters-on-the-half-shell
served in the parking lot,
barbecue at the loading dock,
bottles of expensive champagne
sunk to their shoulders
in pails of shaved ice—just as you
would have done.

Could you see how everyone's
expression changed—
that shift around the eyes,
the inhale—as they realized
whom I held. Your little boy
reached for the cookie tray,
and as we passed
what had been your office,
could you see him turn
and point his chocolate finger.

GRIEF, STILL

The Christmas bread bowl
is hand-thrown stoneware,
20 inches across,
weighs almost 10 pounds.
I've got it in both hands
as I slide it from the cupboard,
rise to set it on the kitchen counter.

And just then—
so fast and sudden
no time no interval
for mind to manage
the onslaught—

>   for a moment you are
>   right where you always were
>   remembering what I'm remembering:
>   this bowl and the dozen Christmas breads
>   we'd make every year.

>   For a moment I think
>   that I will see you soon
>   and tell you that I remember
>   and you will smile and catch my eye
>   with that mix of hope and knowing.

Stillness now,
the moment closes
and I'm sifting flour.
Same recipe.
It has always turned out well.

I LIVE ALONE NOW

I have felt you
reach across me
for the wine glass
on the table

seen the switch
flip
just as the hall light
flickers

heard the scrape and crackle
of the stylus on old vinyl
when you play my records
in the middle of the night.

Sometimes in the evening
as I watch the fire die away,
the shadows jump on the hearth
and climb the chimney stones.

Then you come creaking
up the back porch steps
to *zing* your fingers
along the screens.

I clear my throat, part my lips
to speak. My loneliness rises

from the empty chair
across the hearth,

goes to the back door,
reaches
but fails
to swing it open.

TIMES LIKE THIS

The wind on the pond
circles back on itself
raising crosshatched ripples
that catch the sun and flash
such blinding brightness
you have to look away. Then the wind steps

off the pond up into the trees,
strums them into
their sighing song,
leaving the pond
with the untouched sky
laid out upon its surface. Red-tailed hawks

are jousting above
the fallow fields
filling the lapis air
with their canny scree.
They've seen it all before.
Past years, past lives. Mown hayfields

lie satisfied, settled,
ready yet again
for winter's killing touch.
The last of the cicadas stutter
and whine high in the sycamore
where big yellow leaves flap. Times like this,

if you can step
away from your self,
you can see all of time at once
shot in a single instant
along the horizon.
Everything you've ever known sparking at once

telling the whole story—all of it.
The red-tails, still circling,
cry "grief, grief."
And that's true, but so is
the watery sky at your feet
and the words the trees are singing.

II. SKIMMERS

...the lift and glide...

STILL DON'T UNDERSTAND

Today, the sudden
appearance of an osprey,
her call empyreal
against the emptiness
of a summer drought sky.
But there are only
stagnant farm ponds here
nothing fitting for
her heedless plunge
her wicked talons
her fierce delight.

Close, elusive
she is in the dark pines
edging the pasture. Hot sun
stirs the pines' sweet scent
with a reedy breeze
a branch bows under her weight
she calls again silencing
the nervous yard birds.

Is this you—triumphant and wild—
come back again to show me
that I still don't understand about death?

AND YET

Winter solstice has come and gone
yet mornings seem darker still.
The cedars lean in carefully,
holding extremities close
like old women on icy errands
that cannot wait for a thaw.

Even the trumpet vine—
tough guy of the fence row—
has curled into itself
like the furry souls
that are sleeping down deep
in the meadow grass mounds.

And yet

in the slough beyond the orchard
slips of maple have swelled their buds,

and the bluebirds have turned up
the neon glow of their sun-glinting blue.

Where can I go,
how should I turn,
which way face
to catch the message the maple hears
in the winter storms whistling round the field?
To feel the thrill of sweet nothings
whispered in the bluebird's ear?

THE GEESE ARE BACK

January found me sour with blaming,
raw with the need to fix
you, and sometimes me.
In February, I raged against regret.
It tangled and pinned me down,
tore my hands with its thorns.

Then one day
I hung the sheets out on the line,
and a lone goose flew over
speaking in her wild tongue.
And then I remembered.
Oh—winter. It's only darkness
that has hemmed me in.
And now the geese are back.

If there were some sort of
journal-in-the-sky, each year
I'd record the falling in of my heart,
and the beat and lift of wings.
Then on long winter nights
I would read my words and remember:
Yes, yes. This too.
Be still with even this.

WINGS OF OWLS

are said to be silent
so I can't say
what tipped my head back
made me look up.
Dawn was stepping
through the field.
I was watching to see
what sort of day it would be.
The owl flapped once
circled twice
landed at the roof's peak
panned its head side to side.
Then it reached
and dropped toward me
and in that instant
I wished
for the rake of talons
the pull and lift
of wings.

DROUGHT

The pond
has gathered up its hems
and retreated to its center.
I squat on hard cracked mud
and ask the mild willows
if it will ever rain again.
They wave in the heat shimmies,
waiting. On the mud flats

a heron
moves
slow as
the turning
of the earth
one gnarled foot
then the other—
hunting frogs
that have gathered
in the waning shallows.

SKIMMERS

Forty years
I've scanned the sandbar
across North Inlet in April
and here again are the skimmers
whose light touch of mandible
connects the sky and sea
I come here just for that—
the grace of this connection

forty years of apprenticeship
to those swift black wings
that hardly need to beat the air
that only seem to stroke the water

to the flashy orange bill
gleaning on the wing
in the roiling green shallows

forty years to make a life
as holy as this

but I'm still tethered
to these binoculars
this sandy shore
no forty Aprils
left for me
I let the binoculars hang
kneel in the sand
reach and lean
with the lift and glide

BIRD WOMAN

I dreamed last night
that I could fly,
a little touch-and-go at first
but gaining strength
as I found a rhythm
and caught the wind just right.

As my feet lost touch with earth,
some wild thing
stirred and woke inside me—
what I'd mistaken
all these years
for fear.
It rose in my breast,
its own first flight,
and leapt from my mouth—
a cry of belonging
of finally fitting
effortless
against the sky.

WOOD DUCK CALLS

at first light
a single piped query
from somewhere
in the mist
that chimneys
off the pond

        if I am there
    vapor   dew   blade   feather
    flying from the drake's throat
        as he clears
        the marshy edge

then that call
carries every word
ever spoken

that flight
every question
and the answer

...it must be all right...

THINGS NOTED ON THE WAY TO TOWN

The farm lane I pass down slowly on my way to town,
waves of cornflowers rising and breaking on either side.

The righteous manure spreader
abandoned beside the fallen-in barn.

The sag and slump of the barn as it kneels

in the field gone to weeds and cornflowers.

The grain of the rust on the barn's caving roof,
how it steadfastly refuses to reflect the light.

The way the vultures blink from the barn's skewed peak.

Their jaunty plie' as they rise from the broken ridge pole
and float out over the field, twisting their heads on rubbery necks.

Their satin wings that beat the air and flaunt their sheer white linings
as they pitch and yaw in the updraft

then slide off my windshield view, and disappear behind the tree line
as I pass slowly down the farm lane on my way to town.

IT MUST BE ALL RIGHT

Something dark and quick
just surfaced on the pond.
There's the wind—
a big high sound in the pines.
And these crickets
saying zip-zip, zip-zip
down low in the bleached winter grass.
        So it must be all right.

If the Indian grass
is dabbing the air
with its fronds of seed,
if the marsh hawk
is laying down her benediction
along the slough, surely
        what we've done is not so bad.

The auburn haze of the redtwig hedge—
would it speak so boldly
against the grey tree line
        if it were not all right?

And the juncos. Would they have arrived
in such numbers
on the same day in November
as last year
if it were not, after all, okay—
        what we've done?

I've heard the great horned owl
again this year, faint
and further to the north
now that the woods to the south
have been clear cut.
But I hear her
if it's sharp cold
in the dead of night.
        So it must be all right.

WAITING FOR THE KINDLING TO CATCH

Slivers shaved
from seasoned
hickory
placed over
last fall's beech
leaves—each leaf
tried between
my thumb and
forefinger
for quickness.

The one match
is drawn with
prayer across
the strike patch.
Yellow springs
hungry for
fuel. I am
so often
cold with you,
burrow in
to draw your
body heat.
We both wait,
each making
the other
the keeper

of that flash
of sulfur.
The flame licks
carefully
along the
curling leaves
then touches
the kindling.

DOWN TO THE BONE

There's a bench
in the woods out back,
crouched out of sight
in a bowl of sweet bright mosses—
Thuidium delicatulum, Bryum argentium—
their green unmitigated
their plushness uncanny
here where winter
seems to scrape
everything down to the bone.
Liverworts cling
to the steeper slopes
and lichens are scattered
in scaley patches.
Heaps of oak leaves—
copper, dun, pewter,
and variously curled—
have drifted
against the rotting bench.
I can see where the deer
have been bedding
in a spinney of saplings.
A sapsucker taps
the maple up slope.

The sun has just set.
I know by the chill
that rises from the creek
like a dog rising
at the sound of intruders.

Once, in a parking lot
strewn with sooty remnants
of pushed up snow,
I watched a man in a car
whip a little boy with his belt.
The man sat in the driver's seat,
reached behind
without turning or looking
and lashed and lashed.
He watched himself
in the rear view mirror.
The boy had a buzz cut
and a dirty face.
He disappeared onto the floor.
The belt leapt up into view
and down, then up again
and down and up.
The windows were open
despite the cold.
The boy made no sound.

ADDRESSING CLIMATE CHANGE

Down here in
the little creek bottom
spindly bare maples
poor sparse cedars
honeysuckle
just beginning to leaf
the afternoon light
watery, still thin and
tinny like a distant
signal.

Yet, there is
some warmth
to be had from
the angling sun
it leans in
at my back
then recedes
as the chill breeze
sifts down the slope.

One chorus frog
strums
its rising scale
then the creek muck
wakes and pulses

with 100 more
then silence
for a while
till the one
strums again.

This is not
about life or death
or hope or despair.
It's about being
in the woods
one afternoon
in February.
That's all.

AGALINIS

The first edgy day of autumn
I walk out by the lake.
The power line right-of-way
still tumbles headlong
down to the water's edge
the way it did
when I was a young woman
when the dam was first sealed
and the lake was made.

The fields have grown up in loblolly now,
but the old tobacco rows still rise and fall
just out of sync with my stride.
A red-tail wheels and cries.
Buzzards tilt and slide across the sky.
I push through hip-high
broom sedge and beggars tick
that bounce and sway in my wake.
Then I look up

and see myself across the ditch
standing in the old road bed—
a young woman struck dumb
by Agalinis—
by a profusion of rose and yellow
trumpets nodding on their thready stems.

She dares not pick them
or even touch them.
They cannot bear
her heavy human touch.

She looks at me
and I see what she knows
about time—
time to stand by this ditch
time to come back again and again.

She looks at me
but she does not see what I know
about time—
that I will come back
but only a time or two
and not in September
when the Agalinis blooms.

That decades will pass
until finally I will step
across this ditch again, reach
but pull back
to spare the Agalinis
my heavy human touch.

LETTER TO A GREAT GRANDSON

If I prayed that you would never be born, it was because
        I thought you should not have to bear
Spring without the *wooping* of foxes
        hunting in tandem
Summer without the heron confronting the black snake
        over a half-swallowed frog, or
Fall with no persimmon blume, no sourwood flare,
        no muscadine sweet on the tongue
Winter with no gaunt coyote pawing the edge
        of the frozen pond,
and no hickory smoke with its sweet assertion
        that the wood shed is full and all is well. But
if you are never to know this kind of love,
        maybe there will be no regret.
This is what I could not know as I held your father's little hand
        by the pond, and he startled against my leg
when the wood duck flashed and cried
        rising from the marshy edge.

WHAT'S LEFT

I believe in snapping turtles in farm ponds,
in weedy vacant lots and power cuts,
in successional forests
       of scruffy pine and no-account gum
          healing over clear-cut scars.
In peepers in muddy ditches,
in buzzards riding updrafts,
in fence rows of honeysuckle and privet.

I believe in getting up at dawn
just to see the herring gulls
feeding on the reservoir.
Nothing endangered, nothing rare,
just what,
       after all this wear and tear
       this taking and using
       and having,
is left. I believe in it.

...to let go every single thing...

FIELD WEEDS, WINTER COMING

Brittle scales cling to bare stems,
summer's petals gone to winter's
paper vessels, holding seeds
against what's to come, or for it.

Just a field weed,
this one quivers,
holds its quivering, holds it
till it is sheer vibration.

Holding still while holding all
that can ever happen.
Staying still to hold every single instant—
to let each instant go—
to let go every single thing
that can ever happen.

HICKORY

I am pressing (as I often do)
my cheek
into the steadfast
trunk
of an old hickory
tipping my head
back (scraping my cheek)
to take in
the reach and arch of
limbs above me
I close my eyes (trees don't see)
and think 100 years
and I long for
that intimacy
year after year
with the air
each exquisite part (oxygen, vapor, and sharp nitrogen)
but all I can hope for (tiny human)
is to hold still
enough (for a moment)
to feel the wind stir
our leaves

ABSCISSION

She whispers over her shoulder—
      something of
          redness
          and readiness
          to rot—
to the wet black oaken finger
that has taught her
all her green life.
Then, fetching her petiole
along behind her,
she steps out
onto the air
dips, recovers, dips again
then bears into the curve
of a slow spiral.

WOULD GO, TOO

Mid-winter sunset
Cold gold rim of this Earth bowl
Mind flies to the rim

Body stays behind
Holding the darkening fields
The trees turning black

Fragile human shakes
Tender human would go, too
Foxes bark and run

WILL NOT TELL

I know something that I will not tell.
It sleeps and wakes
down deep
where stones so old
they've known the stars
shape rooms appointed with shadow
and licks of light.
Where there's music so sweet
that ghosts 'round the room
swoon and sway,
smiles on their lips
their heads thrown back.

Old women in robes
who tend the fire
down there
hold hands and point
up toward the opening
high in the wall
where sometimes
the stars come down
and converse with the sparks
that rise from the fire.
Where sometimes
a hawk will pass
in the heat of the day,
calling down to the women
news of the season.

And I will not tell.
Nor will the old women,
nor the ghosts,
nor the stars, nor the stones.
I will not tell
because my tongue
is thick with human-ness.
And the women won't tell
       nor will the fire
              nor the sparks,
                      nor the hawk,
because they know better.

ONE SINGLE THING

Late March of a quintessential spring.
Need I say more about last night's freezing rain
or how this morning turns in a gusty wind
like a suspended crystal. Elusive warblers
shift and flit in the privet. Business-like creepers
journey up and down the hickory limbs. And,
because I have stopped here and let these things
soften at their edges and become one single thing,

all the scratchy facts of the day—the plumbing leak,
the stray cat, the lost password —have been brushed
away like crumbs from my lap. How could this be?
I don't know but I'll take it—this one single thing—
carefully down the trail keeping my gaze soft,
my breath even, my step light, to see how long it holds

how close it comes
how deep it settles.

POTATOES AND SPARROWS AND WIND

Scrubbing the sack of potatoes
brought from the neighbor's farm,
rubbing away the grit and sprouts
with my thumb. This winter's
first snow storm abating.

Earlier, when the snow rushed down the sky,
I walked into the storm, and the wind
stung my face and my lungs.
I stepped into the lee
of the oldest pine on this farm.

So many birds, all tiny and quick ,
were sheltering there
in the closeness of clustered needles.
If I could tell you one thing
and know that you would hear it

I would tell you of potatoes
and of sparrows and wind. I would say
make your life what you want
right now before you're old like me
because it doesn't get easier.

Now the flakes no longer fall but drift and muse
outside my kitchen window. I'll spread
some millet seed for the birds and study
the cryptograms they leave in the snow
while the wind erases it all.

SWEET COMING APART

I could die on a day like this.
The light is November—slow and slanting,
the mild air such a pleasure on winter skin,
the occasional breeze
charged with the tatting and clacking
of sycamore leaves that will hold on
a little longer.

The red-tails are through
with their arduous getting
and raising and fledging.
They wheel and scree,
cruising for field rats.
Beyond them there is nothing
but blue and blue and blue.

I could step away from myself now
with no regrets about
the frost that will come
and reclaim the fields tonight,
or the woodpile wanting,
the lantana unpruned.
I can see from the duff in the woods,
from the hay in the field,
that it would be a gentle parting.
And if I were to long for any of this here,
it would not be for long.

If you can stay still with a day like this,
let out your breath, open your palms to this,
then the particular bundle
that is here and now
is just one season's glory. No loss.
Only this waning light,
then falling, darkness,
and the sweet coming apart.

REMEMBER THIS:

that you walked toward the waxing moon's
neap tide as it laughed and roared
up from the ocean floor

that the green—no, the blue—no, brown...
leapt and tore at the beach
as you came

that it was October—the month that throws you
down, prostrates you before its galloping bent towards
rot and darkness

that an osprey beat and pined against the wind,
tilted and tilted, showed you her white throat
then was driven down so close you caught her gaze.

Remember that you had been old until then—
held, until then, to your words
and your bones.

And remember that while you stood at the top of the dune
the tide turned and each wave
held the light   a little longer

and no one's words mattered any more.
They'd all been said and none of them
was the tide or the light or the osprey's flight.

ACKNOWLEDGMENTS

Mount Hope Magazine, 2017: "Haunt"
New Millennium Writings, December 2015, Issue 24: "Remember This"
North Carolina Literary Review, 2014: "It Must Be All Right"
North Carolina Literary Review, 2017: "Do You Know"
Pinesong, 2010: "I Live Alone Now"
Spillway Poetry Magazine, No. 23, 2015: "Wood Duck Calls"
Third Wednesday, Spring 2012: "What's Left"
Third Wednesday, Summer 2013: "Drought" and "Waiting for the Kindling to Catch"
Third Wednesday, Fall 2013: "Field Weeds, Winter Coming;" "Sweet Coming Apart;" and "The Geese Are Back"
Third Wednesday, Fall 2015: "For Now"
Third Wednesday, Winter 2016: "Coyote Brings Dawn;" "Mergansers;" "Snow Coming"
Third Wednesday, Winter 2020: "Calf"
Turning Point, Spring 2019: "Skimmers"
Via Regia, 2015: "Wings of Owls."
Xanadu, 2011: "Will Not Tell"

ABOUT THE AUTHOR

Joanie McLean (joaniemclean.com) is an ecologist and poet who lives, works, and writes in Silk Hope, North Carolina. She grew up in Wilmington, Delaware mucking about in the creeks and woods along the Brandywine River. Her family spent summers on a lake amidst the woods of central Maine where she first came into the thrall of the natural world. Joanie is co-owner of Mellow Marsh Farm, a native plant nursery, where she grows over 200 native species for water quality and conservation projects. She holds degrees in Botany from UNC - Chapel Hill and in Wetland Ecology from Duke University. She has published two chapbooks, *Place* and *Up From Dust*, is the winner of the New Millennium Writings Prize for Poetry, and a three time finalist for the James Applewhite Poetry Prize. Her poems have appeared in many journals, including *The North Carolina Literary Review, Mount Hope Magazine*, and *Spillway Magazine*. She is currently working on a collection of poems relating her experience with long term Covid-19.

www.ingramcontent.com/pod-product-compliance
Lightning Source LLC
Chambersburg PA
CBHW021448070526
44577CB00002B/306